Mysterious Matters

Story by

Grandma Andee Georgiou

In the beginning...

...there was

There was nothing but silence

and a tiny piece of mysterious energy...

It was so small, it may have been smaller than a single grain of sand.

It was packed **very** tightly together

And it was **very, very, very**

HOT.

Hotter than anything you could **ever** imagine.

One day
this mysterious energy

EXPLODED!!

We call this the

BIG BANG.

But really, there was no 'bang'.

In fact there was **no** noise at all
because there was **no air**.

And without air there is no noise.

All of this happened in silence.

We believe this is how our **universe** began.

In those early few seconds of time,
all of the **elements** and the **particles** that make up

life and you and me

were everywhere.

After the universe had cooled down,
they started coming together.

The next important step was

GRAVITY.

It pulled together those very new particles and atoms
to help create the **stars** and **planets**.

Gravity holds things together;
it keeps our **sun**, **moon**
and **planets** orbiting
in the correct order.

It keeps us upright on **earth**,
and pulls the fruit
that falls from the tree
down to the ground.

Today, the universe still has all of these left-over particles and gases from the silent 'bang'. A new

mysterious

discovery known as **dark matter** makes up 85% of our universe.

You cannot see this dark matter, because it is invisible.

The other 15% that you can see is called **ordinary matter**.

Every element found inside the **core of a star**,
as well as all those created in the big bang explosion
are the **same** ingredients that make up

YOUR WHOLE

BODY.

YOU ARE MADE OF THE STUFF OF STARS!

In fact, you, the earth, the plants

and everything around you was first generated in the stars.

So from this silence, everything evolved.

You are a child of the
UNIVERSE!

You are a star...
YOU ARE AMAZING!